A STREET THROUGH TIME

ILLUSTRATED BY STEVE NOON
WRITTEN BY DR ANNE MILLARD

DORLING KINDERSLEY
London • New York • Moscow • Sydney

Contents

DK

A Dorling Kindersley Book

Project Editor Shaila Awan
Art Editor Diane Thistlethwaite
Deputy Managing Editor Dawn Sirett
Managing Art Editors Peter Bailey
and C. David Gillingwater
Production Ruth Cobb
Jacket Design Dean Price

Published in Great Britain by Dorling Kindersley Limited,
80 Strand, London WC2R 0RL

14 15 16 17 18 19 20

Copyright © 1998 Dorling Kindersley Limited, London

A CIP catalogue record for this book is
available from the British Library

ISBN 0-7513-5535-6

Colour reproduction by Dot Gradations, UK.
Printed and bound in Singapore by Tien Wah Press.

See our complete product line at www.dk.com

THE STORY OF A STREET

SOME STREETS AND EVEN SOME WHOLE TOWNS ARE VERY NEW. BUT THERE ARE SOME TOWNS AND STREETS THAT ARE VERY old. Come with us and explore an old, old street. You will see how it has changed from a camp of nomadic hunter-gatherers, into a settled village, then a town, and then a city. Its progress has by no means been smooth! Sometimes the people living there have enjoyed peace and prosperity. At other times they have faced war, sickness, and poverty. Some buildings in the street have survived, while others have been rebuilt many, many times. You'll find out too, how people's way of life and standard of living have changed – not always for the better!

THE STREET'S INHABITANTS

| 10,000 BC | 2000 BC | 600 BC | AD 100 | AD 600 | AD 900 | 1200s |

A RIVERSIDE SETTLEMENT

The river is central to the story of our street. Some 12,000 years ago it drew Stone Age hunters, pleased to have a good water supply and a handy source of fish! About 4,000 years ago, when farming had replaced hunting as a way of life, the river provided water for people, animals, and crops, as well as fish to eat. Later the river brought trade to the village, helping it to grow and prosper. But the river sometimes brought troubles, too, such as invaders and disease. You can trace the changing role of the river from age to age as the story of the street unfolds.

CHANGING TIMES

For hundreds of years people farmed and lived in the village by the river. They slowly began to cut down the trees that covered the land, using them for fuel, to make tools and weapons, and as building materials. The farmers' lives changed only slowly until the arrival of the Romans caused a total upheaval! By about AD 100 the village had become a town with all the benefits of Rome's comfortable way of life. The local people lived in small flats and traditional huts, while the Romans occupied villas and large houses. Everything changed again when Rome's Empire was invaded by barbarians. The town was destroyed, our street became part of a small village, and people's standard of living plummeted. The struggle to survive and prosper began anew. But it was to be shattered again, this time by Vikings in AD 900.

FROM VILLAGE TO CITY

Eventually powerful kings and lords put an end to the Viking threat. Traders who now sailed up the river helped the village to grow into a town. By the late 1600s the town had survived plagues and wars, though the castle was reduced to ruins. But the real changes came in the late 1700s and early 1800s. Improvements in farming methods meant more people could be fed by fewer farmers on less land. Inventions brought the Industrial Revolution to our street, which was now in a rapidly growing city. There were new industries, new methods of transport, and new wealth. But for some life became even harder.

THE STREET TODAY

Our street remains in a city that has survived wars and spread so far that all the old forests and farmland have disappeared. The pace of change has become so rapid that people who lived in our street only 150 years ago would not recognize the modern businesses along the riverbank. People are much better off now than their ancestors. But what will happen over the next 100 years?

THE TIME TRAVELLER

This is Henry Hyde. He is hidden in the pictures of each historical period. Henry works in a museum, but he has a secret: he has a time-machine. He can travel back to the past and see how people lived and how the objects, now in his museum, were used.

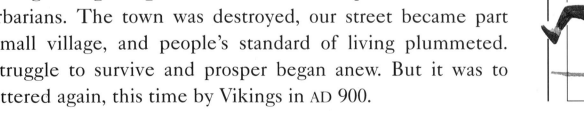

| 1400s | 1500s | 1600s | 1700s | EARLY 1800s | LATE 1800s | TODAY |

STONE AGE HUNTERS (10,000 BC)

Once upon a time, everyone lived by hunting, fishing, and gathering food. People were nomads, moving across the land in small groups seeking food and shelter. This tribe has just found a place to spend the winter. The camp is the start of our street.

Deer skull (symbol of the woodland god)

Preparing animal hide

Chopping wood

Gathering berries

Priest

Storyteller

Fishing

Can you spot the woman using a leather bag to carry water?

Find the old woman telling children stories about the tribe.

4

The animals' meat is eaten, their fur and hides make clothes and tents, and their bones make tools.  Some of the meat is dried and stored, ready for the winter months.

The canoes are made of logs.

Dogs are the only animals people have tamed. Find the dogs fighting over food scraps.

Animal hide tent

Cutting meat

Flint worker

Hunters

Making a fire

Plucking a duck

Making a canoe

Tools and weapons are made of flint. This flint worker has found a good source nearby. The tribe's priest is calling on the spirit of the forest to bless the new camp.

FIRST FARMERS (2000 BC)

More than eight thousand years have passed and people have learned how to grow crops and keep animals. They have also developed new skills, such as pottery making, weaving cloth, and metalworking. The site by the river now has a permanent settlement with huts.

Village dead are buried in a barrow. Can you see it?

Can you spot the man who has just returned from hunting a deer?

Stone circle

Using a bow and arrow

Thatched wooden hut

Hunter

Palisade

Pottery kiln

Wolf

Threshing

Winnowing

Spinning Weaving Sewing

Harpooning fish

6

Wheat and barley grow in the fields. The crops are cut with a sickle made from a sharp piece of flint. The people believe that this goddess makes their crops grow.

Barrow

Cutting crops

Cutting
firewood

Roasting meat

Grinding
wheat

Making a basket

Blacksmith

Metal mould

Making flint tools

Find an old man teaching his grandson how to use a bow and arrow.

Spot the blacksmith busy making bronze tools.

7

 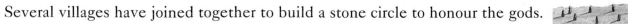

THE IRON AGE (600 BC)

Hundreds of years pass. People have now found out
how to smelt iron to make better tools and weapons.
The village has prospered, but there are battles with
neighbouring tribes, who are fierce rivals.

Ancient
stone circle

Sacred grove

Enemy
heads

Cattle

Rival warriors

Food
hut

Thatched
wooden hut

Palisade

Loom

Pottery kiln

Fishing

Foreign
trader

Tattooing

Wooden boat

8

To help people farm, a more efficient plough has been invented with an iron plough shear. The potter has built his kiln away from his house because of the risk of fire.

Priests offer captured enemy weapons to the gods by throwing them into the river. After the warriors and the priests, the blacksmith is the most important man.

Can you find three wooden statues set up to honour the gods?

Spot two monuments in the hills from earlier times.

Fort

Ancient barrow

Guard

Chief

Thatchers

Ploughing

Prisoners

Blacksmith

Priests

Coracle

Carpenter

A rival tribe has arrived to steal the villagers' cattle. This is a foreign trader. He has sailed up the river. The villagers are eager to buy his wine, silverware, and pots.

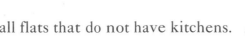

ROMAN TIMES (AD 100)

The Roman Empire has spread across much of Europe, bringing a new way of life. Our village has become a town with hundreds of people. The town has large stone buildings, and a bridge has been built across the river for the first time.

Statue of Jupiter

Temple

Ancient stone circle

Small flat

Carpenters

Wall paintings

School

Domus

Bedroom

Bedroom

Barber's shop

Pottery shop

Baker's shop

Tavern

Toilet

Atrium

Kitchen

Stove

Slaves

Local hunter

Wooden bridge

A rich family lives in a town house, called a domus. The domus has beautiful statues and paintings.  In the amphitheatre, gladiators often fight to the death to amuse the crowd.

Most hard work is done by slaves. Find a batch of slaves arriving.

Find the local chief visiting a Roman official.

Native huts

Fort

Roman soldiers

Amphitheatre

Basilica

Bath-house

Wine warehouse

Crane

Brick building

Fountain

Imported wine in amphorae

Merchant ship

The fort is where Roman soldiers are stationed. They drill and march, so they are always ready for action. Merchant ships bring goods such as wine from all over the Empire.

THE INVADERS (AD 600)

Barbarians have swept across Europe, destroying the Roman way of life. A group have settled in the ruins of our town. All the Roman comforts, such as baths and piped water, have been forgotten.

Ancient stone circle

Columns from Roman temple

Wolves

Sheep pen

Shepherd boy

Thatched wooden hut

Chief

Weaving

Laying fish traps

Wooden boat

Can you spot the ruins of three important Roman buildings near the settlement?

Find a woman weaving inside a hut.

12

The simple huts are made of wood. The chief has the biggest hut. Wood is used for cooking, heating, and building. Find five people chopping or gathering wood.

Wolves have taken a sheep. The shepherd boy tries to drive them away with his sling. Who has found a Roman statue?

Roman fort

Ancient barrow

Roman amphitheatre

Chief's hut

Food stores

Dried meat

Beggars

Blacksmith

Carpenter

Vegetable patch

Slave woman

Washing clothes

Coracle

Sticks are used to make wooden fences. This stops the sheep from straying. 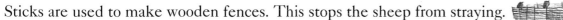 Pigs roam through the village, scavenging. This one takes a bite out of the laundry!

VIKING RAIDERS (AD 900)

The barbarians have now been settled for hundreds of years.
They have become Christians and have grown prosperous. They have
a king who gives his orders through the local chiefs. Now a new danger
has appeared – fierce Viking raiders seeking booty and slaves.

Ancient
stone circle

Hole for fire smoke

Stone
church

Graveyard

Toilet

Viking
longship

Viking

Count the villagers escaping to the woods.

Spot a person hiding in a barrel, another under a table, and another under a basket.

14

 The village has some outdoor toilets. A very awkward place to be caught in a raid! An iron cooking pot can be a good weapon! This family may just be able to escape.

The chief's bodyguards put up the best defence, but most villagers try to run away from the raiders. Unlike the huts, the church is built of stone and will not burn easily.

Ancient barrow

Chief's hall with wooden roof

Thatched wooden hut

Sail rolled up

Jetty

The priest hopes his prayers will drive back the raiders. Can you find him?

Spot the man trying to save his cows.

The church has gold and silver ornaments that attract raiders, but its books are likely to be burned. The people flee. Women and children will be taken and sold as slaves.

MEDIEVAL VILLAGE (1200s)

More than three hundred years have passed. The king has given the land to a lord, who has built a castle to protect the people from Viking raiders. The lord uses mounted warriors, called knights, to race to trouble spots. In return, most people have had to give up much of their freedom.

Ancient stone circle

Common land

Spire

Fallow land (unplanted)

Glass windows (used by the church and rich only)

Church

Peasant's house

Cobbler's shop

Baker's shop

Villagers use the common to graze sheep and cattle. Can you see this land?

Find the entertainers in the marketplace.

Reed cutter's boat

16

Villagers grind their grain in the lord's mill. They think the miller keeps some of their flour! The village has three fields. Each villager has strips of land in each field.

The villagers live in small houses. Their animals are often stabled in part of the house. Today is market day. Some people have come from other villages to buy and sell goods.

The lord's wife is buying cloth from a foreign merchant. Can you see them?

Can you spot the travelling dentist?

Stone castle

Keep

Castle wall

Windmill on site of ancient barrow

Miller's house

Barley strips growing

Wheat strips growing

Chimney

Knight's stone house

Timber-framed house

Inn

Dentist

Milkmaid

Blacksmith

Pedlar

Foreign merchant

Sailing boat

17

A ball game with boys from the neighbouring village is turning into a rowdy riot! It is cheaper to bring goods by river and safer, too – there may be outlaws in the forest!

MEDIEVAL TOWN (1400s)

Thanks to the trade brought by boats up the river, the
village has grown into a town. Its citizens have purchased
a charter from their lord. This allows them to run the town.
Some of the merchants have become very rich.

Church

Collecting
firewood

Wine merchant's
house

Bedroom

Doctor

Shutter

Cobbler's shop

Weaver's
shop

Baker's shop

Religious
procession

Kitchen

Merchant lending money

Selling wine

Cellar

Stone bridge

Can you guess what the inn is called from the sign outside it?

Find the doctor treating his patient by bleeding his arm.

Household waste gets thrown into the street. Who is in for a nasty shock? Rich citizens can afford to have expensive glass in their windows and an indoor toilet, of a sort!

Stone castle

Turret

Miller's house

Windmill

Town guard

Deer hunters

Gibbet

Guildhall

Tapestry

Glass window

Market cross

Inn

Armourer's workshop

Stocks

Black rats come off the ship

Foreign merchant's ship

Lord and his wife return from a visit

19

Petty thieves are placed in the stocks, and the gibbet is used to hang murderers. Craftsmen have formed guilds. These unions protect the craftsmen and set standards of work.

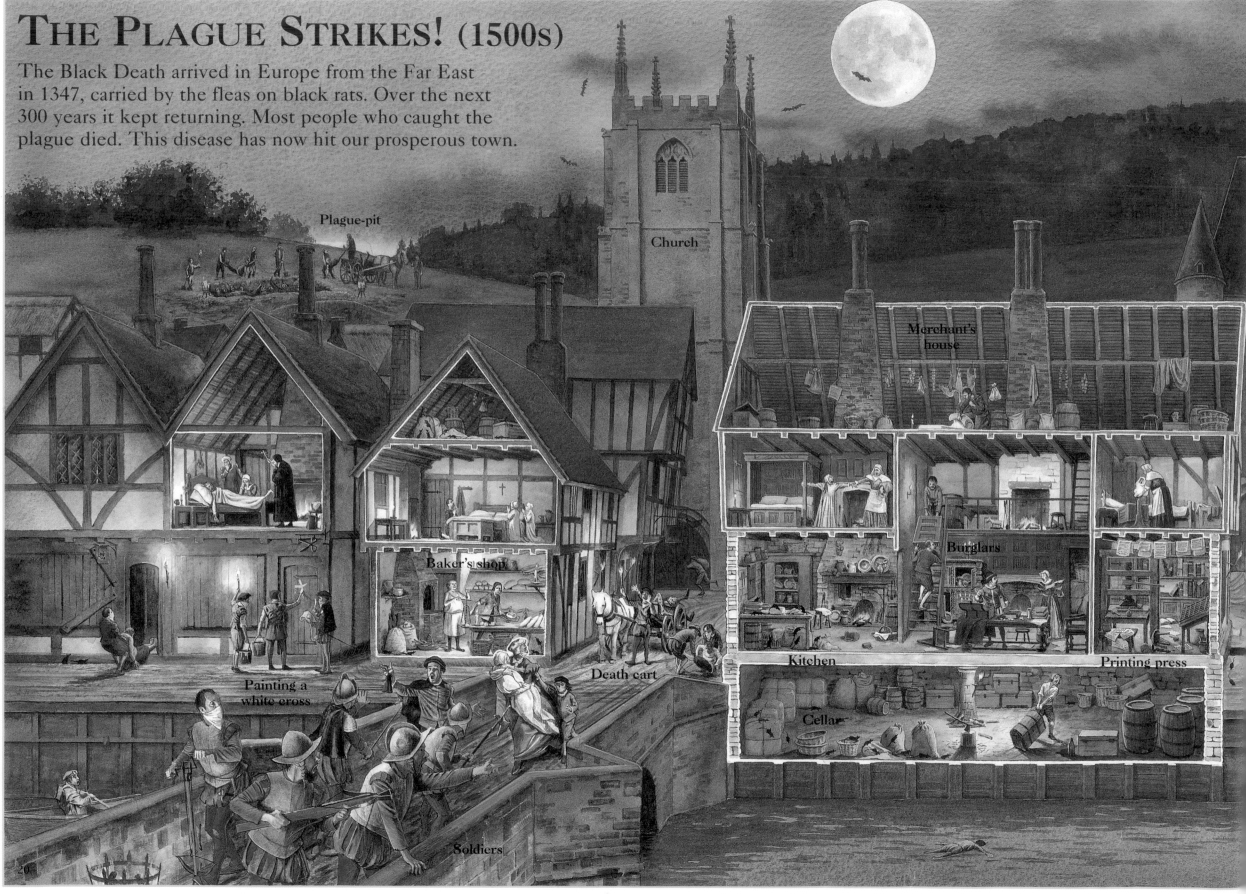

THE PLAGUE STRIKES! (1500s)

The Black Death arrived in Europe from the Far East in 1347, carried by the fleas on black rats. Over the next 300 years it kept returning. Most people who caught the plague died. This disease has now hit our prosperous town.

Plague-pit

Church

Merchant's house

Baker's shop

Burglars

Death cart

Kitchen

Printing press

Painting a white cross

Cellar

Soldiers

How many people have died in the streets? Black spots under the arms were a sign of plague. Who has just found some?

A cart collects the dead and takes them to a plague-pit where the bodies are buried together. The open sewers in the streets attract the rats. They are everywhere now!

Stone castle

Miller's house

Windmill

Gibbet

Guildhall

Inn

Apothecary's shop

Doctor

Escaping by riverboat

A white cross on a door shows there is plague inside. No-one can leave the house. The doctor wears a strange mask, hoping this will stop him from catching the infection.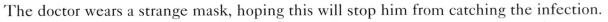

UNDER ATTACK! (1600s)

War has broken out. The people are fighting over religion and about who should rule the country. The castle and town are both under attack, and the townspeople are losing! Not even the castle walls can withstand the pounding of the improved cannons.

Enemy soldiers

Church

Cobbler's shop

Tailor's shop

Cobbler's shop

Kitchen

Merchant's house

Printing press

Town soldiers

22

Find the soldier and his wife trying to escape on horseback.

Two people are hiding under a bed. Can you see them?

Some people climb on to the roof of their house, hoping that they can escape from the enemy.   A soldier has been hit by a falling shop sign while trying to flee from the enemy!

Guns, called muskets, are in use. They fire only one bullet, then have to be reloaded.

Cannons have been around a long time, but the new ones are more powerful.

How many buildings have been set on fire by cannonballs? A brave woman has decided to fight back. Can you see her?

Stone castle

Windmill

Miller's house

Doctor

Stone house

Inn

Cannon

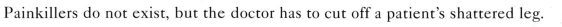

Painkillers do not exist, but the doctor has to cut off a patient's shattered leg.

The innkeeper is being threatened with a pike, a nasty weapon carried by foot soldiers.

AN AGE OF ELEGANCE (1700s)

Peace has returned and the town is prospering again. Some houses have been repaired, while others have been rebuilt in the latest style. The wealthy citizens have a lot of spare time. They pride themselves on their polite manners, their learning, and their elegant parties.

Spire

Church

Clock

Servants' bedroom

Servants' bedroom

Wife's bedroom

Husband's bedroom

Reading poetry

Playing cards

Dancing

Sitting-room

Laundry room

Kitchen

Brick building

Shoe shop

Dress shop

Wig shop

Milkmaid

 A mailcoach speeds out of the inn. These coaches carry passengers as well as mail from town to town. Some people sell fruit, flowers, and other goods in the busy street.

Find the statue of the previous lord, who defended the town. Find the rat-catcher. No wonder the plague has died out!

Squire's house

Castle ruins

Lord's mansion

Inn

Guest-room

Highwayman

Guest-room

Town hall

Bar

Mailcoach

Statue

Stagecoach

Hat shop

Coffee shop

Sedan chair

Rat-catcher

Chimney-sweeper

Sailing boat

25

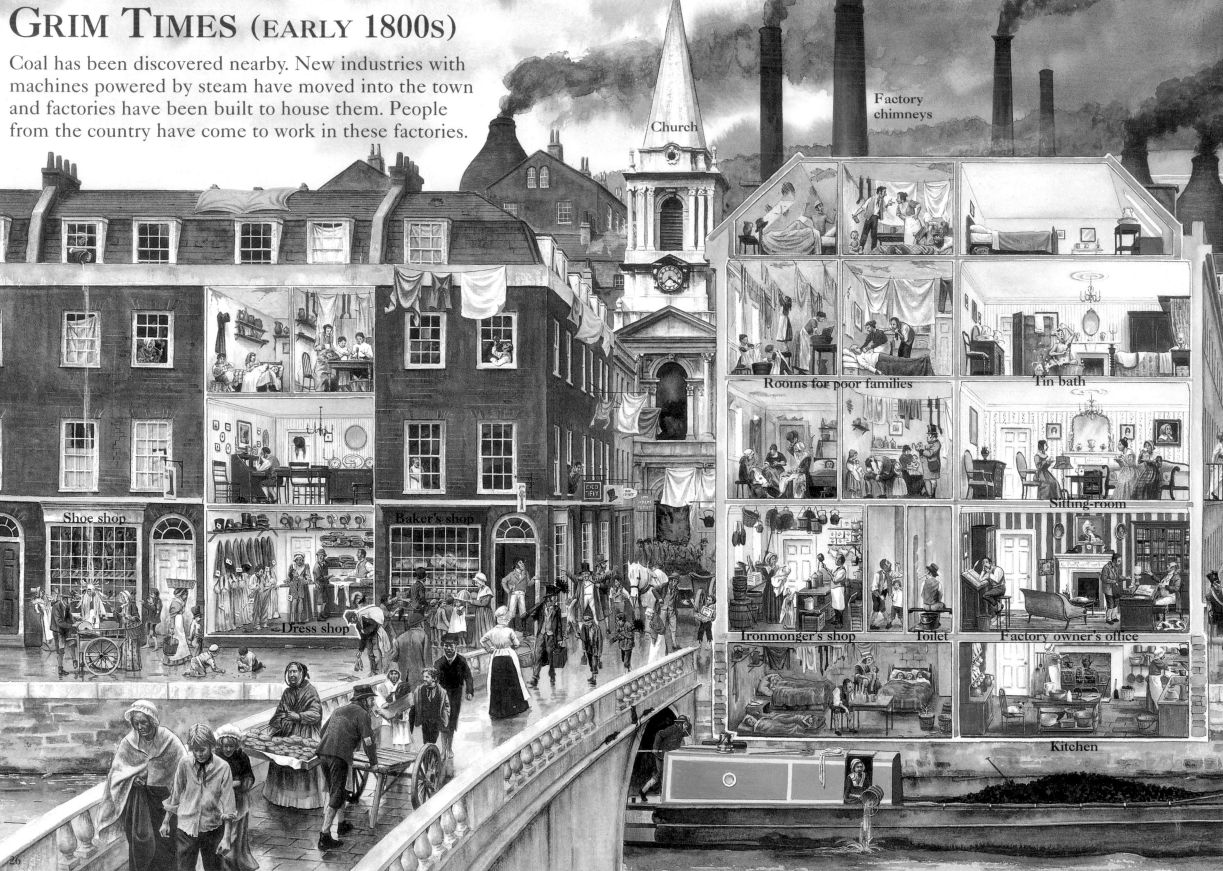

GRIM TIMES (EARLY 1800s)

Coal has been discovered nearby. New industries with machines powered by steam have moved into the town and factories have been built to house them. People from the country have come to work in these factories.

Factory chimneys

Church

Rooms for poor families

Tin bath

Sitting-room

Shoe shop

Baker's shop

Dress shop

Ironmonger's shop

Toilet

Factory owner's office

Kitchen

Find the man whose roof is leaking. Most houses are crowded. Can you find the house in which only one family lives?

Poor children have to work too, so that they can earn money. Most cannot read or write. There are no homes to look after orphans. Some live and sleep in the street.

A few brave men are experimenting with a new form of travel. What is it? Who cannot sleep because of noisy neighbours?

Hot-air balloon

Castle ruins

Coal mines

Pottery kiln

Gambling

Pick-pockets

Town hall

Inn

Liquor shop

Pawnbroker's shop

Milk cart

Orphans

Coal barge

With the overcrowding, the dirt, and polluted water many people become ill. Some people drink to forget their misery. This drunk is in danger of falling off the roof!

Rich families have bathrooms. Can you find a bathroom?

Police now help to keep order and fight crime.

FROM TOWN TO CITY (LATE 1800s)

Thanks to its industries, the town has grown into a city. Many people are better off, and working and living conditions have improved. A new railway line now begins in our street and carries people and goods to other towns or cities.

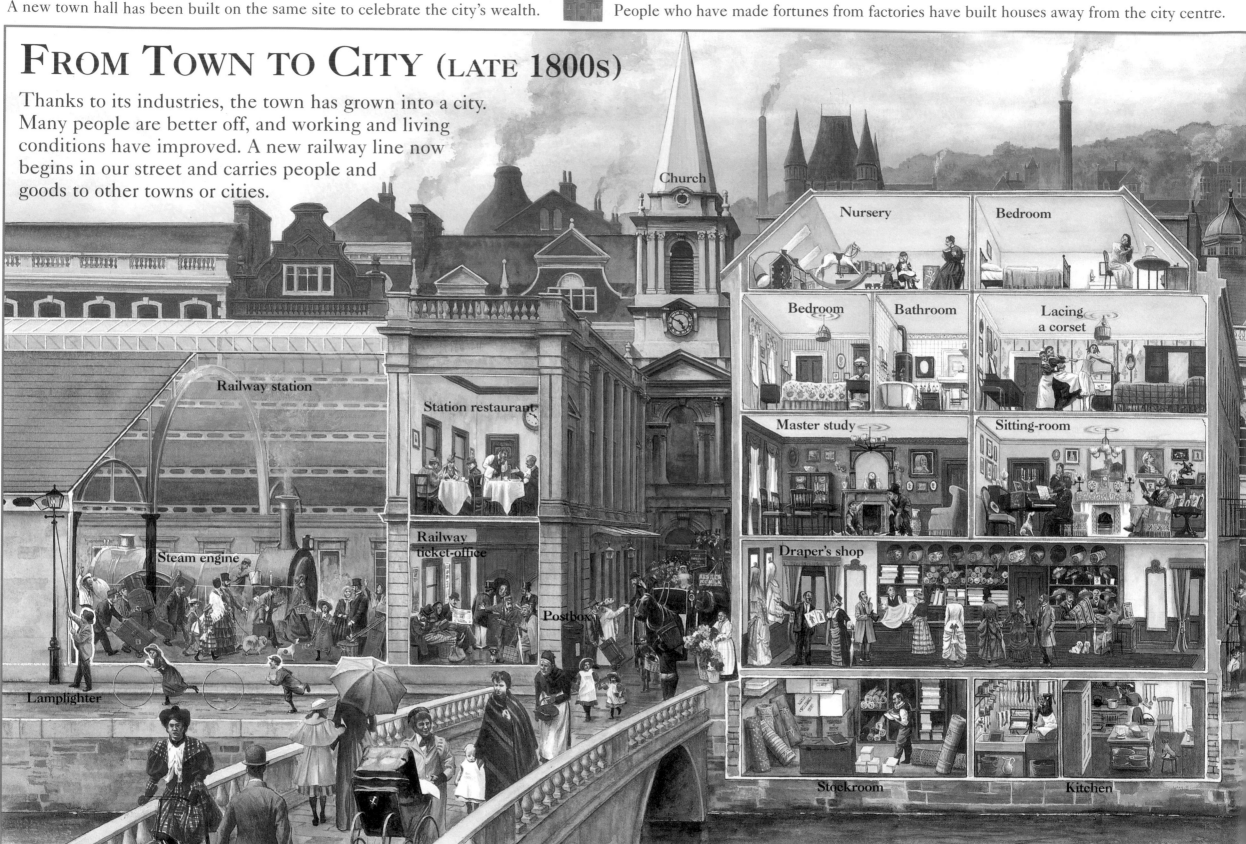

Church

Nursery

Bedroom

Bedroom

Bathroom

Lacing a corset

Railway station

Master study

Sitting-room

Station restaurant

Railway ticket-office

Postbox

Steam engine

Draper's shop

Lamplighter

Stockroom

Kitchen

28

Growing suburbs

Castle ruins

Factory chimneys

Town hall

Guest-rooms

Inventor

Restaurant

Omnibus

Public bar

Saloon bar

Shoe shop

Inn

Toy shop

Road sweeper

Cellar

Steam pleasure boat

Photographer

A cheap postal service has been set up. Where do people post their letters? Who is being taken for a run by her dogs?

THE STREET TODAY

In recent years there has been much change in our city. Modern businesses have replaced most heavy industries, people have become more environmentally aware, and leisure time has increased for many people.

Crane

Office block

Flats

Hairdresser's shop

Artist's studio

Church

Dentist

Bathroom

Solicitor's office

Café

Bookshop

Bank's office

Museum

Museum shop

Clothes shop

Bank

Safe

Gymnasium

Jogger

Rowing boat

Spot new forms of communication, such as a TV or phone.

Men dredging the river have found a chest. Who dropped it and when?

30

 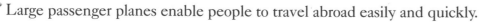

Many people who work in the city live in houses or flats that have been built around it. The river is used for leisure activities, such as rowing.

Why is the bank manager in for a nasty shock? A crane is being used to construct a tower block. Can you see the crane?

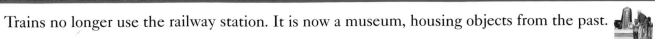 Trains no longer use the railway station. It is now a museum, housing objects from the past. There is a smart new town hall. Look how much glass has been used to build it!

TIME-TRAVELLING QUIZ

Below is a list of some of the things Henry Hyde has seen while visiting all the periods in our street's history. Can you find these things too?

STONE AGE HUNTERS

The hunters start a cooking fire by rubbing two wooden sticks together. Find the man using this method.

FIRST FARMERS

Reeds growing near the settlement are used to make baskets. Can you find the woman weaving a basket?

THE IRON AGE

Can you see the warrior being tattooed? Vegetable dye is used to paint the patterns on his body.

ROMAN TIMES

A crane is used to lift heavy building material. It is worked by slaves. Can you find the crane in the street?

THE INVADERS

Find two different wooden boats used by barbarian tribes.

VIKING RAIDERS

The local people are now all Christians. Find the graveyard where they bury their dead.

MEDIEVAL VILLAGE

Important buildings are now made of stone. Can you find three stone buildings?

MEDIEVAL TOWN

What structure has been built in stone across the river?

THE PLAGUE STRIKES!

With a printing press, a book only takes a few days to print. Find the press that has been abandoned during the plague.

UNDER ATTACK!

Refuse and sewage is still dumped in the street. Spot two places where it is trickling into the river.

AN AGE OF ELEGANCE

Can you find the highwayman examining his loot from a recent raid?

GRIM TIMES

Two children are playing a game of marbles in the street. Can you see them?

FROM TOWN TO CITY

There is now a new toy shop in the street. A boy is busy choosing a toy soldier to buy. Can you find the shop?

THE STREET TODAY

How many of the objects in the museum can you find in earlier periods in the book?

32

GLOSSARY

Amphitheatre (page 11*): An oval or round building with seats. Used by Romans for wild beast shows and gladiator fights.

Amphorae (page 11): Clay jars with two handles. Used by Romans to keep wine and other liquids.

Apothecary (page 21): A person who makes and sells medicine.

Atrium (page 10): A central hall in a Roman house with the rooms opening off it.

Barbarians (page 3): Romans referred to people who lived outside the Roman Empire as "barbarians". In particular, the word is often applied to people from north and northeastern Europe who began invading the Empire after AD 200.

Barrow (page 7): An old form of grave, consisting of an earth mound over burial chambers.

Basilica (page 11): A Roman building. Law cases and other town functions were held there.

BC and AD (page 2): BC means years *before* the birth of Christ. AD refers to the years *after* the birth of Christ.

Charter (page 18): A written document given by a king or a lord granting rights to someone.

Coracle (page 9): A small oval boat made of woven sticks and covered by a waterproof material.

Domus (page 10): A Roman town house used by a wealthy family.

Gibbet (page 19): A wooden gallows where dangerous criminals were put to death by hanging.

Guilds (page 19): Unions of craftsmen or merchants that controlled working standards, conditions, and prices. They also cared for members in trouble.

Guildhall (page 19): A place where guild members met to run their guilds and the town.

Industrial Revolution (page 3): A period during the 1700s and 1800s when there were huge changes in the way people lived and worked. This was brought about by new inventions that led to factories producing goods faster than people could at home.

Iron Age (page 8): Although people were experimenting with iron by 1100 BC, the period of history known as the Iron Age began about 900 BC, when iron replaced bronze for making tools and weapons.

Jetty (page 15): A landing place on a river or in a harbour.

Keep (page 17): The strongest part of a castle was the stone building, known as the keep.

Nomads (page 4): People who wander from place to place seeking food and shelter.

Palisade (page 6): A fence of strong wooden poles built around a fort or village to help defend it from enemies and wild animals.

Roman Empire (page 3): About 200 BC Rome began conquering other lands and created an empire that was to last in western Europe until AD 476. At its height, it covered much of Europe, North Africa, and parts of the Middle East.

Sling (page 13): A piece of leather or woven material used to hurl stones.

Stocks (page 19): A wooden frame with holes for feet, neck, and hands. It was used to punish small-time crooks.

Stone Age (page 3): A very long period of history when tools and weapons were made mostly of stone. It began when the earliest people made their first tools and lasted until metal was introduced.

Sulphur (page 20): A yellow mineral that burns with a choking smoke and horrible smell.

Threshing (page 6): Beating grain with flails (special sticks) to get the grain out of the ears.

Winnowing (page 6): Tossing grains into the air to separate them from their light cases.

Vikings (page 3): Fierce warriors from Norway, Sweden, and Denmark. They raided and settled in parts of Europe between AD 700 and 1100.

*Note: The page numbers refer to the first page on which the word appears.